Yellow Umbrella Books are published by Capstone Press
151 Good Counsel Drive, P.O. Box 669, Mankato, Minnesota 56002
http://www.capstone-press.com

*Library of Congress Cataloging-in-Publication Data*
Rubin, Alan (Alan Adrian)
  Fast and faster! / by Alan Rubin.
    p. cm.—(Science)
  Includes index
Summary: Briefly describes how animals and vehicles move in different
ways and at different speeds.
  ISBN 0-7368-2018-3 (hardcover : alk. paper)
  1. Speed–Juvenile literature. [1. Speed.] I. Title. II. Science
(Mankato, Minn.)
  QC137.52.R83 2003
  531'.112–dc21
                                                                2003000925

**Editorial Credits**

Mary Lindeen, Editorial Director; Jennifer Van Voorst, Editor; Wanda Winch, Photo Researcher

**Photo Credits**

Cover: Gary Sundermeyer/Capstone Press; Title Page: Comstock; Page 2: Flat
Earth; Page 3: DigitalVision; Page 4: Comstock; Page 5: Steve Mason/PhotoDisc;
Page 6: DigitalVision; Page 7: DigitalVision; Page 8: Corbis; Page 9: Corbis; Page 10: DigitalVision;
Page 11: DigitalVision; Page 12: Jim Schwabel/Index Stock; Page 13: DigitalVision; Page 14:
Corbis; Page 15: Defense Visual Information Center/U.S. Air Force Photo; Page 16: DigitalVision

1 2 3 4 5 6 08 07 06 05 04 03

# Fast and Faster!

by Alan Rubin

Consultant: Dr. Paul Ohmann,
Assistant Professor of Physics, University of St. Thomas

Yellow Umbrella Books

an imprint of Capstone Press
Mankato, Minnesota

# Some things can't move at all.

# But you can!

# Some things move slowly.

# Some things move faster than others.

# This animal can move.

# But this animal can move faster!

# This animal can run.

# But this animal can run faster!

# This car can go.

# But this car
# can go faster.

# This train can go.

# But this train can go faster.

# This plane can fly.

But this plane can fly faster.
What goes even faster?

# Rockets go faster! Zoom!

# Words to Know/Index

**animal**—any living creature that can breathe and move about; pages 6, 7, 8, 9

**car**—a type of passenger motor vehicle; pages 10, 11

**faster**—moving at a greater speed; pages 5, 7, 9, 11, 13, 15–16

**go**—to move away from or toward a place; pages 10, 12, 13

**move**—to change place or position; pages 2, 4, 5, 6, 7

**plane**—a machine with wings that flies through the air; plane is short for airplane; pages 14, 15

**run**—to move along quickly using your legs; pages 8, 9

**rocket**—A vehicle shaped like a long tube with a pointed end that can travel very fast; page 16

**slowly**—moving at a low speed; page 3

**Train**—a string of railroad cars; pages 12, 13

Word Count: 77
Early-Intervention Level: 7